Winning Your Traffic Crash Injury Claim In Illinois

Guidelines For Success With Your Illinois Vehicle Accident Claim

Scott Blumenshine, Attorney at Law

ISBN: 978-1-941645-30-7

Designed and Published by:

Speakeasy Publications

73-03 Bell Blvd #10

Oakland Gardens, N.Y. 11364

www.SpeakeasyMarketingInc.com

(888) 225-8594

Disclaimer

This publication is intended to be informational only. No personal legal advice is given, and no attorney-client relationship is created by reading this material. If you have a legal claim, you may need to consult with professional legal counsel to get your questions answered and retain a counsel if action is needed.

Scott A. Blumenshine

Chicago, IL

(312) 263-1000

sbshine@mbpersonalinjurylaw.com

www.mbpersonalinjurylaw.com

CLIENT TESTIMONIALS

"I couldn't have made a better selection of an attorney to represent me. Scott Blumenshine really took matters into his hands and always made me feel my case was truly important. Genuine, respectful service. I am very happy and glad that a friend recommended this law firm to me. Thank you for everything Scott." **- H.R.**

....

"I am very pleased with the services I received from the firm. I always knew that Scott was looking out for me and my best interests with his tireless pursuit of justice. Thank you, Scott and team. I will always remember how you made it right for me. You keep your promises." **–B.W.**

....

"I have never been involved in a lawsuit and was hesitant, but could not be more pleased that I get the medical treatment for my injuries, as well as a settlement for all the other expenses. Highly recommended." **-K.T.**

....

I just wanted to say thank you very much for all your efforts and determination that you had Scott. Thank you for not giving up on me when everyone else did. I could tell that you had compassion for my case, you saw how my leg injury really affected me. And for that, I thank you. Thank You for putting yourself in my shoes and realizing how bad this thing really was. The hard work you and your team did will never be forgotten. Thank you from me and my family." **- M.B.**

TABLE OF CONTENTS

Traffic Crash Injuries and the Insurance Claim

Commercial Vehicle Collisions

Uninsured, Hit and Run and Underinsured Motorist Claims

Attorney Introduction

Scott Blumenshine's professional mission is to obtain prompt and fair payment of claims. Personalized, strategic, compassionate service helps to achieve that goal. He believes in the duty given in Proverbs 31:8: "Speak up for those who cannot speak for themselves, ensure justice for those who are being crushed."

Scott has recovered millions of dollars in compensation for clients through settlement, mediation, arbitration and trial. He listens to your story and your concerns and answers your questions. He and his team work together to best present your claim. They then work to achieve a fair and timely result.

Mr. Blumenshine has invested in improving the legal system for the public. He writes on current legal issues and addresses fellow lawyers at continuing legal education seminars. He has authored Illinois Insurance Code amendments which increased penalties against insurers for Insurer Bad Faith Delay and Denial. Other legislation he authored increased limits for binding arbitration awards on Uninsured and Underinsured motorist claims.

Mr. Blumenshine has been a voice in the legal system regarding significant public safety dangers. He has been interviewed and provided commentary on TV for many high profile cases. He has also been quoted in articles regarding Illinois insurance law.

Handling Auto Accident Cases

I have represented hundreds and hundreds of people in their injury claims over 28 years of law practice. As everyone is unique, every case is different and a challenge. It is a pleasure to meet, represent and work with every single client.

"Handling" a claim means doing everything required from beginning to end. The beginning of a case is our initial meeting which can be in person, by phone or through email exchanges.

We listen to your story, ask questions, and ask you what you need from us. We gather evidence about the incident including reports, videos, photographs and witness statements. We often visit and photograph the scene, vehicles and injuries. We then collect medical records and bills and prepare and deliver a settlement demand to the other party. The demand is done with your agreement. We attempt to reach a prompt and fair settlement with the insurance company. If the insurer is not reasonable, then we file a lawsuit in court.

A lawsuit involves ongoing action including court appearances by us, taking sworn deposition testimony, collecting records, drafting and filing legal documents, and strategizing on how to succeed with your case.

We also resolve cases through negotiation, mediation, arbitration, pre-trial settlement conferences with judges, and, if necessary, jury trials and appeals. Our team handles your case until it is resolved.

Is an At-Fault Driver Financially Responsible for All the Damages in an Auto-Accident?

Yes. A negligent driver is responsible to compensate an injured person for all their injuries. In almost all cases, the driver's insurance company is responsible under the insurance contract. That's the purpose of insurance.

The injured person is entitled to recover what the law calls "damages." Damages are compensation for your injuries. Compensation is intended to make you "whole" or to "balance the scale of justice." Damages include financial losses like medical expenses and lost income, as well as non-financial losses such as pain, suffering, disability and disfigurement. Damages are all the consequences that result from being injured.

Pain is the physical symptom of your injury - a broken bone or torn ligament will cause pain. To be free from pain is valuable. To suffer pain is costly.

Suffering is the mental and emotional anguish that comes with the experience of your physical pain.

Disability is the inability to function like you did before the accident. You do not need to be bedridden and unable to move to have "disability." You can be partially disabled. Examples of disability are weakness or limited range of motion in your back. Other examples of disability would be headaches that limit your concentration, or stiffness in your neck that hinders your ability to do computer work for long periods of time.

Disfigurement is a visible physical injury such as scarring or bruising.

One way to think about damages is the phrase "Harms and Losses." If you've been seriously injured, you'll have harms and losses. The driver who causes an accident is responsible for compensating you for those harms and losses.

OPTIONS FOR PEOPLE INJURED IN A VEHICLE ACCIDENT

The options for someone seeking compensation from an at-fault driver are:

1) Simply do nothing and have their health insurance or their auto medical insurance pay their bills,

2) Make a claim against the other driver's insurance on your own and see what happens,

or

3) Get an effective attorney on their side.

Insurance companies are masterful at delaying and denying claims. An injured person is at a disadvantage when they try to handle a claim on their own. Insurers have billions of dollars, thousands of staffers, and the incentive to drag out the claim process. If insurance company marketing messages were true, insurers would

quickly and fairly pay everyone what is due. That is not what happens for most valid personal injury claims. Unfortunately, you do not have unlimited time and resources to fight insurance company resources on your own.

Representation by an experienced and capable attorney is usually necessary if you have a serious injury. The legal system has extensive, complicated rules and procedures. A good attorney knows court rules and procedures *and* also has the skills to effectively present your claim. A layperson could find and read court rules and procedures somewhere online. But to put the case in motion and bring it to a successful conclusion is a major undertaking.

The claims process typically has two stages. The first part is the demand for settlement. Successful negotiations may or may not happen when this demand is first made. If settlement isn't reached, then the second stage is filing a lawsuit in court. A lawsuit raises the stakes. It requires that specific rules are followed and detailed procedures are done properly and timely.

We often receive calls from people who have attempted to handle their claim or lawsuit on their own, but they have found they are unable to properly proceed. We would be glad to help you if you have reached a dead-end in handling your claim on your own.

When is a Personal Injury Lawsuit Necessary?

A lawsuit has to be filed if your claim is not settled quickly and fairly. The unfortunate truth is that insurance companies usually delay, deny or low ball your claim.

Insurance companies want everyone to think they are reliable, warm, fuzzy and generous. Insurers advertise about how wonderful they are: they put you in good hands, and they're like a good neighbor, and they'll take care of you. However, when a major injury claim is made, they batten down the hatches, they fight and often insult you, they don't pay on-time, and they don't often treat you fairly. We see it every day, year after year.

Now, I understand that I only see disputed claims and it is possible that sometimes insurance companies do pay some smaller cases in a way that satisfies the people affected. The vast majority of cases I have handled, however, involve insurance company delay and denial. When the insurance company does not offer a fair settlement offer, then swift litigation must follow.

Time Limits for Filing an Auto Accident Lawsuit in Illinois

Two years is the standard deadline to file a lawsuit. The time limit is called the "statute of limitations." If a lawsuit is not filed within two years of the incident the right to file suit is lost. There are some exceptions to the two year limit: for example, a child under the age of 18 is not an adult with legal rights that are triggered until they reach 18. Someone who is mentally or emotionally disabled may be considered legally incompetent. Lawsuits against government entities often must be brought within one year. All cases are different, so customized legal advice is necessary.

Do Comparative Fault Rules Apply for Auto-Accidents in Illinois?

Yes. The comparative fault rules apply in Illinois. Comparative fault (also known as contributory negligence) is based on the fact that there may be more than one cause of a crash. To illustrate: in a rear-end collision, almost without exception, the driver who rear-ends someone is 100% at fault. However, in an intersectional collision, both sides may claim they had the right of way. A left turning driver may say the oncoming car was speeding. Who is at fault? Perhaps both drivers are partially at fault. Their fault is compared.

Comparative fault is an important principle. It can reduce your recovery by the percentage that you were at fault. If your injury is worth $100,000, but you were 20% at fault, your recovery would be $80,000.

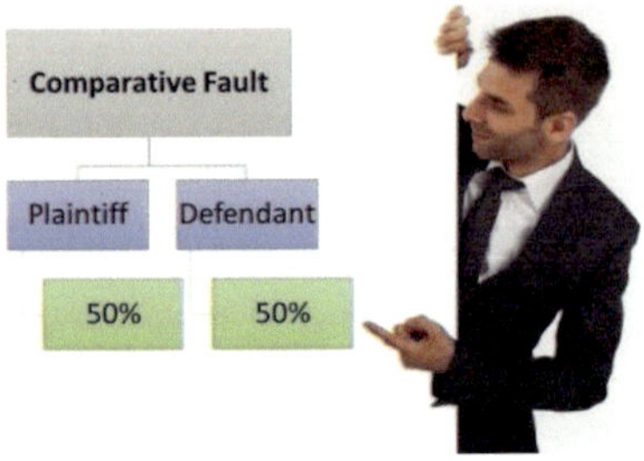

There is no scientific method for determining percentage of fault - it's based on the facts. Thus, your ability to testify in a clear and persuasive manner about what happened will affect how a judge or jury views who is at fault and at what percentage. Most importantly, a capable attorney can show your role in an accident in the most positive light favorable to you and discredit or counter the other party's arguments based on the facts and the law.

CAR INSURANCE LAW REQUIREMENT IN ILLINOIS

Drivers in Illinois must have at least $25,000 in liability insurance coverage. This is a pitifully low amount. It is only enough to pay for minor injuries. If you have a major or even modest injury, $25,000 is not enough to compensate you. Politicians have been swayed by insurance industry lobbyist arguments that higher mandatory minimum limits would make insurance unaffordable for many and there would be many more uninsured drivers.

The law requires drivers to have insurance. Statistics show that many people disobey the law and drive uninsured. For this reason, it is critically important for you to have adequate Uninsured and Underinsured motorist coverage. By "adequate," I mean *at least* $100,000 and ideally $1,000,000 for you and your family.

Many people drive off the car sales lot with insurance and then fail to pay their next monthly premium. They are then "uninsured." This is one example of why uninsured and underinsured motorist coverage is so critical for you and your family. You have to protect yourself, your family and your passengers. If there is one thing you can take away from this book, please do this: *call your insurer and make sure you have at least $100,000 in uninsured and underinsured motorist coverage.* Look into the nominal cost to move your liability limits to at least $100,000. You will be very glad you did so if you ever need it. The cost is not much relative to the amount of the coverage.

Steps to Take in Filing an Auto-Accident Lawsuit

The first thing you should do after an auto accident is to get medical treatment. Whether you go to the emergency room, an urgent care center, or your doctor, you must get medical care. You may just feel a twinge, or discomfort, but small symptoms can be a sign of something serious. So get examined. Follow your doctor's instructions. Take care of yourself.

The second thing to do is to document your claim. Think like an investigator or a police detective and gather every scrap of information you can. Collect scene photos, vehicle photos, witness information

and make notes of the circumstances, such as traffic conditions or something the other driver said or did at the scene. Write down your own recollection of what happened in detail as soon as possible while the events are fresh in your mind. Just as importantly, keep track of ways in which your injury impacts your daily life.

Do not sign anything from the other driver's insurance company. Do not give any statements to the other driver's insurance company.

Shortly after the incident, you should take time to find and speak with a qualified, trustworthy attorney. The consultation must be free and without obligation. This initial consultation should be a valuable experience.

Do not speak with "Ambulance Chasers." They are the attorneys or their "investigators" who illegally swoop down on the scene or the emergency room and pester you in person or by phone. They pay cops and nurses for information. Ethical rules prohibit this conduct. An ambulance chaser is violating the law before they even represent you! Imagine what they might do with your case if you decide to have them handle your claim.

Ask a trusted family member, friend, co-worker or professional for a lawyer recommendation. Search the internet for an attorney who is competent, trustworthy, has great results and good references from former clients. A phone call with an attorney should cost you nothing but your time and will be well worth it, even if you decide to handle your case yourself.

ROLE OF POLICE IN AN AUTO ACCIDENT

The police should be on the scene of an accident. Don't leave the scene without having a police officer come and take a report, no matter how minor the collision appears to be. Some police departments will say they don't come to the scene unless there is a serious injury. If so, go to the police station after medical treatment and file an accident report in person because a police report is critical to protecting your rights.

If you're carried away from the scene by ambulance and taken to the emergency room, contact the police afterwards. Insurance companies like paper, and a police report is documentation that can help protect your rights.

If I am Cited by the Police, Will My Auto Accident Compensation Claim Be Doomed?

No, your case won't be doomed if a police officer gives you a ticket. The ticket is simply the officer's second hand opinion. The facts and the law are what count. Opinions, speculation or guesses by other people

are not admissible evidence. A police officer who did not witness the collision cannot prove that you are at fault without the facts to support his or her conclusion. So do not think a ticket will ruin your claim. Talk to an attorney before the traffic court date.

Police officers are rarely witnesses to the incident. They are usually told after the fact by the parties or the witnesses what happened. There are always two sides to a story. If you know you're not at fault and you didn't cause the collision, refuse to compromise. The insurance company may deny your claim, but experienced and capable legal counsel can help you fight that denial.

ROLE OF INSURANCE IN AN AUTO ACCIDENT

Ninety-nine percent of the time, insurance is the source of any payments after a car crash. That is the purpose of insurance – risk protection. We pay insurance premiums to protect ourselves against risk which the insurance company accepts.

You should always notify your insurer and the other driver's insurer of your injuries. You may be wary of making a claim on your policy for fear of increased premiums or cancelled coverage. However, *notifying* your insurance company about an accident is not the same as making a *claim*. If the other driver is at fault and his or insurer steps up and pays for the property damage and your injuries, you do not need to make a claim against your own insurance policy. But notice to your company is always a good step.

The reason to notify your insurance company is so that you don't lose any rights if you file a claim later. Almost all insurance policies require you to notify your insurance company of a potential claim in a timely manner.

For example, you are in a car accident and the other driver is at fault and uninsured. If you don't tell your insurance company about your injuries and medical bills until many

months after the incident, your claim could be denied for your delay in notification. Your insurer may claim they were prejudiced in investigating the claim.

You may believe that the other driver's insurance will pay promptly. After all, that's what the insurance commercials all promise. If the other insurer does not pay, and you then turn to your insurer for payment, your insurance company may say you failed to notify them in a timely manner. They may claim you deprived them of the right to investigate, and they can then deny your claim.

As for the other driver's insurance company, notify them immediately. Again, notifying an insurer is different than making a formal claim. So, before you give a statement or sign any releases or authorizations, please get an attorney consultation. The consult should be free, with no obligation and is something I strongly recommend.

I have handled many cases in which people unsuccessfully tried to settle cases themselves. People often hurt their case by giving statements or signing authorizations. Be very careful about what information you provide to the other driver's insurance company. The adjuster will sound nice and friendly but - Be Careful – their job is to pay you little or no money and to delay the process.

What to do if the Other Party's Insurance Company Contacts me?

If the other driver's insurance company contacts you, it is okay to verify your identity and that you were injured or had car damage. However, I strongly recommend that you not give any statements or sign any documents. Your statements can be evidence used against you. As you have heard on TV and in movies: "Anything you say can and will be used against you."

You have **no obligation** to the other party's insurance company. You may be in pain, in shock, on medication or simply shaken up from the accident. Then the claims adjuster contacts you. You are in no condition at that time to deal intelligently with an experienced claims adjuster.

Insurance personnel are trained, experienced and knowledgeable about the process - and you are not. You're in no position to reasonably deal with them until after you've had a chance to recover and be prepared. Therefore, before you speak with the other insurance company, get informed and at least speak with an attorney who knows what they're doing.

What if the Other Driver's Insurance Company Denies Liability?

You have two options if the other driver's insurance company denies liability: one is to just forget about it and give up. The other option is to file a lawsuit. While you can legally file a lawsuit yourself, it's difficult, if not impossible, to do it properly.

Therefore, the best option if liability is denied is to retain an attorney who is experienced, aggressive and capable. Find an attorney with whom you're comfortable, who understands what happened to you, who understands your goals, and agrees to pursue a full and fair recovery with you.

Viability of an Auto Accident Injury Claim in Illinois

There are three main elements that make an auto injury case viable.

1) Liability (fault)

2) Damages

3) Insurance

The first element is the liability (also called fault or negligence) of the other driver. The easy example of a driver with liability is a rear-end collision - yes, that driver is at fault. If the other driver is at fault, and you have a serious injury you may have a viable claim.

Liability is not always clear cut. If you have a collision at an intersection, and you know you had a green light but the other driver says they had a green light, this creates a "liability question." If you're the only witness who says you had a green light and other witnesses say your light was red, you have a problem. But if you have witnesses in your favor who also say you had a green light and the other driver had a red light, liability of the other driver exists.

The second element of a good case is a significant injury. A significant injury is one that causes you pain and impairs your life for at least several months. Examples of a significant injury are head trauma, or a back, neck, knee or shoulder derangement that requires extensive treatment. Extensive treatment may include therapy, injections, medications and surgery. The injury will keep you from taking care of yourself. You miss work or school. Significant injuries often have lifelong consequences.

An insignificant injury is something minor such as short term whiplash. For example, your neck is sore for a week or two, but you get better and the soreness goes away. It may seem significant to you and your life, but it doesn't meet the standard of injury of a good case. A jury will not have much sympathy in such a case and the insurance company will thus not offer you much money. You're fortunate from a health perspective if you recuperate quickly, but it will be difficult to recover much in the way of legal compensation.

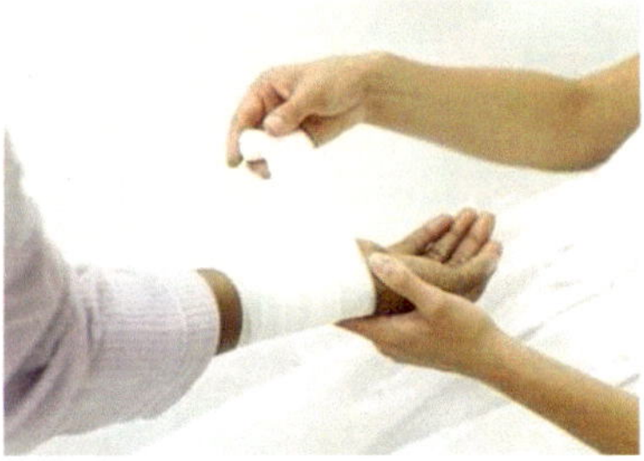

The third element of a viable claim is sufficient insurance. Many drivers have no insurance or low insurance limits. If the person who hits you has little or no insurance, you'll have an uninsured or underinsured motorist case against your own insurance company.

Sufficient insurance is at least $100,000 for a significant injury. Unfortunately, many people drive around with just the minimum $25,000 in coverage. If your bills are over $25,000, their insurance proceeds will not be enough to pay your claims. A viable case has sufficient insurance coverage. Insurance proceeds can come from the other driver's liability insurance coverage or from your own uninsured or underinsured motorist coverage.

To reiterate, the three elements of a viable case are the liability of the other driver, a significant injury, and sufficient insurance coverage with the other driver or with your policy.

Timeframe for Resolution for Auto-Accident Cases

Cases typically take a while to resolve. What is "a while?" A case takes at least three months and often longer. Some cases can take years. Generally, you should not settle too quickly or too early, because you do not know the extent of your injuries until time passes. You must get medical treatment. Your body and mind must heal. That takes time.

Understand that once you settle, you release the other party from any further liability. If you settle too soon, and a year later you still have problems, you're out of luck. It is important to be patient and not settle too quickly.

If a lawsuit has to be filed, the case could take longer than a year. Cook County courts move cases on a fairly rapid basis. Lawsuits typically go to trial within 18-27 months. Although that seems like a long time, it's a great improvement from when cases took 5 or more years to get to trial.

We manage the litigation process to work in your favor. We make the process work by complying with deadlines and requiring the other side to produce evidence by way of testimony and documents. We then ask the court for the earliest trial date possible. This keeps pressure on insurers who like to delay payment.

IMPORTANCE OF MEDICAL ATTENTION AFTER AN ACCIDENT

Immediate medical treatment and proper follow up are crucial. I cannot emphasize this enough - if you are hurt, get medical attention.

If you feel fine, and you have zero symptoms – no twinges, pains or aches, you don't have an injury claim and there's no reason to see a doctor except to confirm that you are ok. However, in my experience, many people say they initially feel "fine," except that they have a little headache or dizziness that later turns out to be migraines from a concussion. You may have had a head injury and you feel "okay," but there could be something going on that could become something serious if not addressed early and properly.

I have seen many people who feel some neck or back soreness, but they don't get treatment. A few weeks or months later, the pain and limitations invariably become worse and they begin to suffer unnecessarily. They have pain that keeps them from doing normal things like sleeping, taking care of chores, and working. But they didn't seek medical attention and do not have a record to show the connection to the accident.

Many conditions turn out to be an injury that seemed minor at first, and because they didn't get early treatment, it became worse. All doctors, chiropractors, orthopedic surgeons and physical therapists say early treatment is preferred. So, if you are fine and you feel nothing, then maybe you are not injured and maybe you don't need to see a doctor. However, if you feel *anything* abnormal, or different, or uncomfortable, get treatment as soon as possible.

How do Delayed Medical Complications Figure in an Auto Accident Claim?

If you wait to see a doctor, the insurance company will argue that you were not hurt at the time of the accident and there is no connection between the crash and your medical condition. The insurer will argue that something else happened to you after the accident, like maybe you tripped or you were in another collision that their insured didn't cause. It's a guarantee

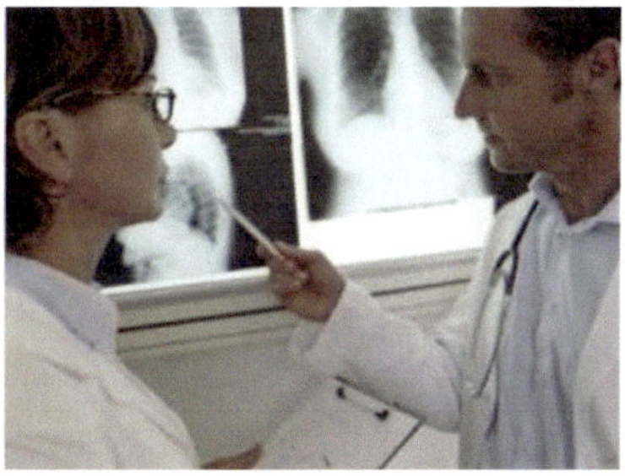

they will make that argument - and it is difficult to overcome. If you don't see a doctor right away, you are handing the insurance company ammunition to defeat your claim.

Many judges and jurors agree with the argument that late or delayed treatment means no injury or minor injury. We have seen it time and again in our own cases and in other cases we follow through the jury verdict reports and settlement reports.

While it is understandable that you don't want to go to the doctor – no one wants to because it's inconvenient and it's time-consuming – for your benefit and the benefit of those who rely on you at home or at work, get the treatment you need now.

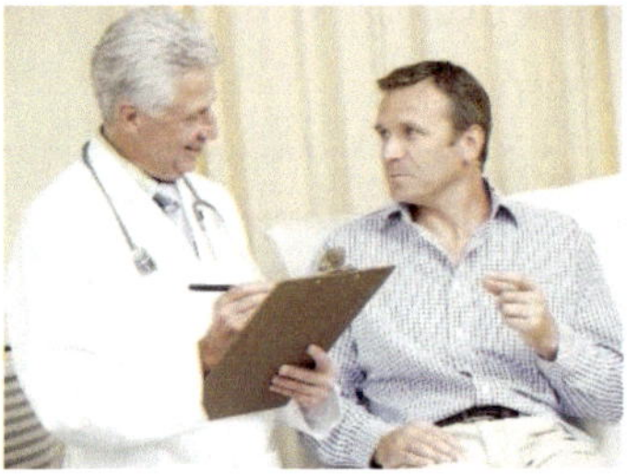

This is about your injury. If you are hurt, you need to see a specialist who can diagnose and treat your injuries first. The claim process and litigation is secondary to your physical health. My recommendation is that you get immediate medical attention if you're hurt. You can address the claims process or legal issues the next day or the week after the incident.

Payment of Medical Bills in an Auto-Accident Case

Ultimately the other driver (through their insurance company) should pay for your medical bills. Payment, however, usually isn't made until the case is settled. Vehicle liability insurance companies don't pay bills as you incur them, they pay at the close of the case. Your case can go on for a year or more after the incident. In the meantime, hospitals, doctors and other medical providers want to be paid. Bills should be paid by your health insurance, or your auto insurer who will later be reimbursed by the other driver's insurer.

If the other driver has no insurance, you'll look to your own uninsured motorist coverage. And if the other driver's insurance isn't enough to cover your medical bills, you look to your underinsured motorist coverage. Uninsured and underinsured motorist insurance are very important sources of protection that is discussed in the last section of this book.

Should I Release my Medical Records to the Other Party's Insurance?

I strongly recommend that you not sign any release of your medical records to the other driver's insurance adjuster. Although you may be told and believe that the release is only for records related to your treatment from the injury, the release will be broadly worded and you may be authorizing release of confidential, private medical records going back to your childhood. Your signed release may include release of private psychiatric records and other things that you don't want disclosed. And, to add insult to injury, the insurer will use your records against you to argue for reducing your payment or for not paying you at all.

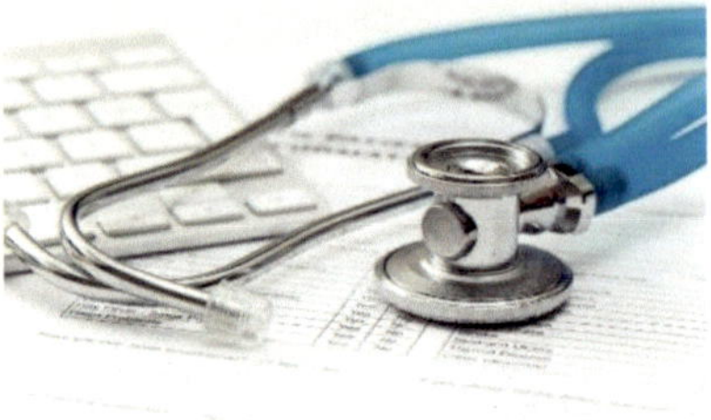

If you do sign a release, it should only be with an attorney recommendation and in the context of a court case in which there is a strict court order prohibiting those records from being released to anyone other than the insurance adjuster for purposes of evaluating your claim.

CAN AN ATTORNEY HELP NEGOTIATE DOWN MEDICAL BILLS?

Yes. Nearly every injury case that we handle includes hospital bills, medical bills and lien claims. And in nearly every case we work on your behalf with lien holders to negotiate those medical bills.

A "lien" is the legal term for the claim that a medical provider or health insurer has against settlement proceeds. The claim is enforced by written notice (a "lien") to an insurance company and an attorney. In most cases we work on the client's behalf with lien holders to negotiate the lien claim. We will contact each lien holder and negotiate the amount they will recover from your personal injury claim recovery.

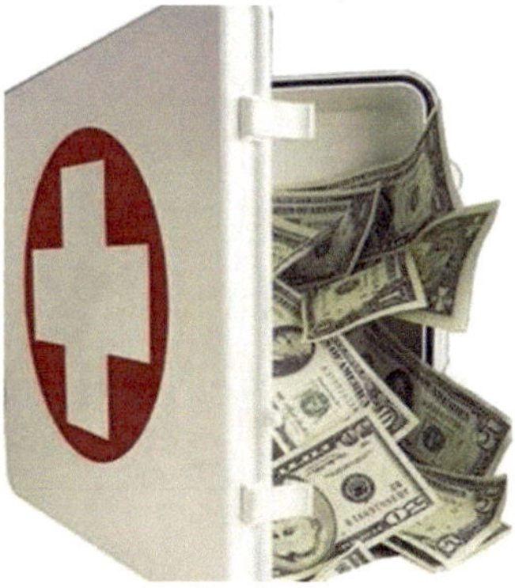

Illinois law limits how much a medical provider can receive from a personal injury settlement, so we're aggressive about getting those liens reduced. If lien holders won't work with us, we'll file a motion in court and ask for a court order to reduce the lien claim.

What if I am Disabled and Unable to Work Due to an Auto Accident?

There are two answers to the question: what happens if you are disabled from work due to your injuries?

One is the practical issue: How do you manage your obligations when you are unable to get around and in pain? Hopefully you're able to get the proper medical and rehabilitation care to get you on the path to healing. Also, if you are lucky, you have family or friends who can help tend to your daily tasks at home.

The second question is a financial issue. How will you survive financially? Hopefully you have some bit of a savings cushion. Perhaps you have disability insurance through a personal policy or through work, and that may provide an income source while you're unable to work until the case settles.

If your injury claim is work related, you will have a workers' compensation claim, which means your employer must pay a portion of your income while you're out of work due to the work injury.

If you have neither disability insurance nor workers' compensation insurance, the next line of resource are savings, friends, or family. Also, lawsuit loan companies are in the business of providing (high interest) loans to people that have filed an insurance claim. We don't necessarily advocate for those loans; if you decide to apply for a loan, however, we will cooperate with the lender in order to assist you in your time of need. Note that the interest rates on those loans tend to be high and you will have to repay the full loan and interest regardless of the amount of your settlement.

Is It Ever Beneficial to Keep a Journal of Events Following the Accident?

Yes. No person has a perfect memory. Claims can take time to resolve and memories can fade. If you are able to record the specifics of how you feel, your experience in dealing with your injuries, your treatment,

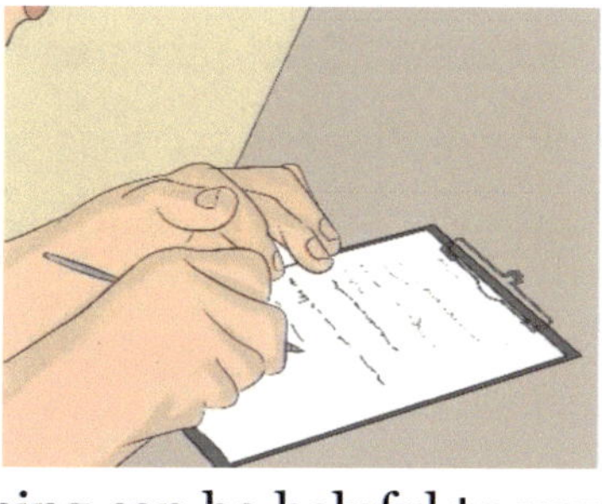

and other information - note keeping can be helpful to you and your attorney. Examples of useful information would be sleep trouble due to pain, struggles with household chores, or anxiety over income loss.

Mark the notes as: "personal confidential attorney-client communication." They will be used solely for purposes of telling your attorney about your experience. Your attorney can then use the information to support the value of your claim. You should share it only with your attorney in order to keep the legally privileged and confidential nature of the document in place. If you share with others, it may no longer be confidential. It is critical to record your experience before your memory fades.

The Importance of Pictures as Evidence in an Auto-Accident Case

"A picture is worth a thousand words." Images can be more powerful and effective than words. So, if you are able, take pictures of the scene and items such as vehicle damage and bruising. Take pictures of any visible injuries you have, and of any devices such as crutches, wheelchair, or other items provided to you. Get the photos to your attorney.

Top Misconceptions Regarding Auto-Accident Claims

The number one misconception about an injury claim among injured people is that insurance companies will be fair and honest in the way they handle your claim. People are usually shocked, disillusioned and disappointed by the insurance claim experience. We are taught from an early age - if you break it, you must pay for it. We are taught ethics and morals as children. We have a reasonable expectation that others will act accordingly.

Insurance companies, however, are typically not guided by morals or ethics. Their motto, it has been said, is “Deny, Delay, Don’t Pay.” Their focus is collecting premiums and not on paying claims.

The law in Illinois does not hold insurers accountable. In Illinois the Insurance Bad Faith laws are weak. I have fought long and hard to have these laws strengthened. We achieved some increase in the penalties years ago, but the insurance lobby is powerful. Consumer friendly states allow for significant fines and penalties for insurer delay.

Insurance companies advertise that they help and protect you. They paint a picture of being a source of warm fuzzies and hugs to make you feel safe and warm. They advertise the "good feelings" and "promises" so that you pay your premium to them year in and year out.

When it comes to paying out substantial injury claims, however, insurers are usually confrontational, dismissive, and slow to pay properly and fully. If insurers were fair, why would people need injury attorneys?

The second misconception people have is that they can handle a significant injury case on their own. You are a smart and capable person, but the arena of insurance claims and litigation is filled with all sorts of rules, and not all of them are logically anticipated. You must meet endless deadlines, follow procedures and implement strategies. The insurance companies have a big leg up on you if you go solo. First of all, they have billions of dollars, claims adjusters, defense attorneys and all sorts of staff to handle these disputes - and you don't. You are walking into a lion's den. The reason you can't handle the case on your own isn't because you're not smart or tough enough. You can't handle a litigated case, because you don't know the rules and you don't likely have the time and money. So you are outmatched without a champion advocate.

A third misconception is that all lawyers are not trustworthy. As in any human arena, there are a few bad apples that spoil the bunch, but in my experience, the vast majority of injury lawyers are trustworthy, honest, hardworking and want to help you. Certainly the lawyer that you choose should have a long established record of ethical, moral and honest behavior, on top of successful results. The best way to find that lawyer is through references and testimonials.

Unintentional Mistakes People Make that Hurt Their Auto-Accident Claim

#1 - Not getting the medical care you need. Many times, people wait too long to go to the doctor. Or, people go to the emergency room and they don't follow up. I understand that it's inconvenient and perhaps scary to go to the doctor, and to therapy, to get injections or more invasive treatment. No one *wants* to do that, but if you have been injured and intend to make a claim, the only way to document the medical aspect of the claim is to get proper medical care.

So get treatment promptly and follow up fully if you are serious about recovering your physical health.

#2 - People can hurt their claim if they don't document and record how the injury has affected their lives. As lawyers, what we say is not evidence - we can't testify, or authenticate photos. We can only use the evidence that is available, including testimony from you and other witnesses like family members and friends, and medical records. If you don't document and record how the injury has affected your lives, your lawyer can't fully prove your case.

#3 - Another way that you can hurt your case is to post on Facebook or other social media. If you post items about yourself and insurance companies, defense attorneys will pick up on that. I was in court the other day and an insurance defense attorney said the first thing they do now is to go on Facebook and try to find statements or photos that suggest the person making the claim isn't really injured.

You probably should stop posting on social media after an injury claim.

How do I get my Car Repaired After an Auto-Accident?

Ideally, the car repair process is simple and the other driver's insurance fairly handles the repair process. They may simply tell you to get an estimate at the body shop of your choice and the repairs will be authorized and completed. Get the authorization for repair in writing. Get pictures of your car and a copy of the estimate and/or repair bill.

Through the other driver's insurance, you should also get a rental car while your car is being repaired, although the key word is "should." If they don't do so, you can request your own insurance to get a rental car while your car is being fixed.

Will Insurance Handle Everything After an Auto-Accident?

Maybe, is the answer. Your bills may have to be paid initially by your health insurance or your auto insurance "medical payments coverage." The other driver's insurance will only make one lump sum settlement payment at the close of the case. In the meantime, your medical bills have to be paid and you are responsible for your bills. Rarely will the at-fault insurer pay your bills as they are incurred.

If you have a minor injury, you can handle the case on your own, but if you have a significant injury in which you're disabled or in pain for more than a couple of months, you'll be outgunned and out-resourced by the insurance company. They have millions and millions of dollars to pay defense attorneys and adjusters and experts and you don't. The insurance industry's hard core business goal is profit. They profit by collecting insurance premiums and then they pay out in claims. Paying claims hurts their profit. Insurance companies' primary purpose is to collect money, invest it and keep the profit. Their secondary purpose is to pay no money or as little money as possible on claims.

So, the playing field is not level. Insurers have unlimited resources (time and money) and you do not. To have a fair chance, you need a capable, aggressive and trustworthy attorney on your side.

Types of Vehicles Typically Involved in Commercial Vehicle Accidents

Commercial vehicles are semis, trucks, vans and other vehicles used for business purposes. Commercial vehicles include trucks of all types, tractor-trailers, vans, pickups, delivery trucks, taxis, and buses. A commercial vehicle could be a UPS or FedEx truck or a food delivery car.

Many collisions are caused by taxis, and, now Uber, Lyft and other ride sharing transportation companies. Any vehicle, truck or car used for business is a "commercial" vehicle. Businesses exist to make money, but businesses are responsible for damages caused by their vehicles used in the course of business. They should, by law, have insurance to cover that risk.

Delivery vehicles have a higher collision frequency, in part, because they must make their deliveries quickly. Drivers can be distracted or drive too fast. Jimmy Johns promises "freaky fast" delivery. That guarantee of fast is certain to cause speeding, crashes and injury.

Our office is in the Chicago Loop. At least half of the vehicles on the road are taxis. Taxis are always shooting in and out of traffic lanes, making overly aggressive turns, and pressing up on pedestrian crosswalks. They are paid to go fast. When they cause injury, they must pay. We often see clients injured by taxis.

Are Commercial Vehicles Subject to Different Regulations and Laws than Personal Vehicles?

Specific laws and regulations apply to commercial vehicles. For example, tractor-trailers that haul loads on highways are subject to federal and state laws regarding truck use and operation.

Owners have to ensure that safe maintenance schedules are followed. Loading must be proper and critical systems like steering and brakes must be regularly inspected. Drivers, according to federal and state law, must inspect their vehicles before and after each trip. Drivers are strictly limited in the number of hours they can be on the road.

Loads placed into trailers cannot be too heavy. That's why you see roadside weigh stations along the interstate. Loads must be secured and balanced so as not to allow for load shifting. There are regulations and laws that affect commercial vehicles and rightly so. Commercial vehicles used for business purposes pose a very significant risk to other drivers, bicyclists and pedestrians who use the roadways.

Common Causes Of Commercial Vehicle Accidents

We live in an age of distraction. Even though the message "Don't Text and Drive" is everywhere, people still text while they're driving. People use other phone functions while driving. Any phone use is a distraction from the primary task of safe driving.

Drivers often talk on the phone while driving. Although this is legal in Illinois, it is distracting. The human brain cannot fully focus on two things at once. A motorized vehicle presents a risk of harm to everyone on the road and it commands a driver's full attention.

Lack of full attention to driving causes collisions. Carelessness is a cause of collisions. Carelessness includes driving too fast, following too closely, making sudden lane changes, disobeying traffic signals, or just simply not paying proper attention.

When a driver of a commercial vehicle is careless, a serious collision can occur. In fact, if you think about it, the two biggest factors in vehicle collisions are improper speed and improper lookout.

Any one of us can potentially cause an accident, but a commercial vehicle, because of its size, can cause exponentially greater injury than a car. If a truck is going too fast, it's more likely to rear-end somebody, run through a light, go through a stop sign and cause an injury. If a truck driver is not keeping a proper look out, there are hazards they may fully see which increases the likelihood of a collision. Many business policies pressure drivers to drive unsafely and that encourages lack of a proper lookout.

Think about the Jimmy John's. Their deliveries are "freaky fast." It concerns me when I hear the radio commercials bragging that their drivers go "freaky fast." When you see drivers with the Jimmy John's signs on top, you have a driver under pressure. They are pressured to get the food to the customer now! The problem is, fast driving compromises our safety. The customer's hunger may be satisfied, but possibly at the expense of someone being injured.

Domino's Pizza used to guarantee 30-minute delivery time. To many of us, that's an outrageous policy, because it encourages drivers to drive unsafely. In fact, the company ended the policy after several major collisions by Domino's drivers caused serious injuries.

When a commercial vehicle causes a collision, the owner and the driver of the vehicle are responsible. Perhaps other companies involved with that vehicle can be responsible. For example, if a company has a fleet of trucks and they hire a maintenance company to do regular inspections, but the brakes weren't inspected on a timely basis and the brakes fail, the maintenance company may be responsible. So it is important that a full investigation be conducted of a claim involving a commercial vehicle.

Can Companies Avoid Liability?

Corporations and insurance companies are masterful at protecting themselves from liability. It is unfortunately true that companies and their individual officers often seek to avoid liability. However, a skilled attorney can work through those legal defenses and help you.

Another way corporations attempt to avoid responsibility is when insurance companies place "fine print" in their policies.

Such fine print includes limitations, exclusions and deadlines in an attempt to not pay under certain conditions. Who reads or understands that stuff? Not the average consumer.

Having an effective attorney working through insurance company nonsense is sometimes the difference between a successful claim or failure. In addition to filing suit against owners and maintenance companies, you must also seek recovery against the driver. Corporate insurance policies typically cover both the owner and the driver.

What Happens if a Driver of a Commercial Vehicle is a Private or Independent Contractor?

Some trucking companies make its drivers sign agreements that say the driver is not the agent of the company. A company and their drivers can set up agreements between themselves, but the law may invalidate those private agreements.

We are a nation of laws. Companies should not be able to avoid liability based on self-serving "agreements" that harm the public.

We seek to hold whomever is responsible for a collision liable. For example, a company can call a driver an "independent contractor" and have the driver sign an agreement saying that. However, if we find that the driver is an agent under the law, we characterize the driver as a legal representative of the company. We argue that the company is responsible for the actions of its agent - the driver. The law can be complex on this issue and it often requires research and investigation, but we enjoy investigating and proving these types of claims.

Difference Between Commercial and Passenger Vehicle Accidents

Business vehicles typically cause more severe injuries because they're bigger and heavier than passenger cars. If you think of basic physics: mass and speed - you know this is true. Trucks are usually larger

and heavier than cars, so the vehicle damage and injury to the person inside a car is almost always worse with a truck crash. If you had a choice, would you rather be rear-ended by a Toyota Prius or a tractor-trailer?

Typical Injuries Sustained in Commercial Vehicle Accidents

We have seen terrible consequences from truck collisions - from paralysis to brain injuries to severe neck and back damage and even fatal injuries. We've seen horrific crush injuries in which cars go under tractor-trailers. We have seen injuries requiring hospitalization and surgeries, and we have seen one client rendered comatose.

We have seen injuries to the "extremities," the legs and arms and all their parts - knees, shoulders and hands. Typically, the injuries sustained in a crash with a commercial vehicle are significant, alter people's lives and require extensive recovery time and treatment.

Steps to Take When Involved in a Commercial Vehicle Accident

Get treatment. Go to the emergency room if in severe or disabling pain, so treaters can rule out something imminently harmful. Next you may choose to go to your family doctor who will likely refer you to a specialist. If you're hurt, you need medical treatment.

The second thing to do is make sure you gather any and all evidence. Record information about the accident, photos of the scene and vehicles, photos of visible injuries, and information about witnesses, your medical treatment and all other helpful information. Gather it together and keep it in a folder for easy access.

Third, get a free consultation with an attorney who knows what they're doing. You should be comfortable with your attorney and feel that you can tell them anything or ask them anything related to your claim.

The Challenges People Face in Commercial Vehicle Accident Cases

There are many challenges in these cases, so allow me to discuss it in two parts: the *physical* aspect of your injuries and the *financial* aspect.

The physical aspect is dealing with your pain and limitations. Our bodies are meant to do wonderful things - to move around, to allow us to work, play and hug our loved ones. When our bodies are subject to trauma, it can take a long time to recover.

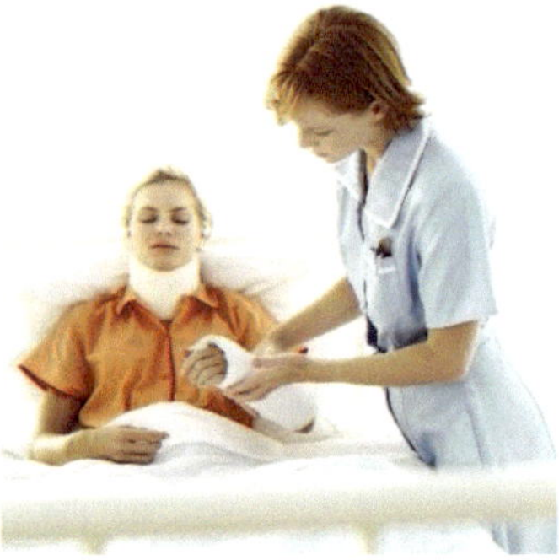

It can be weeks, months or even years before you return to normal.

Dealing with severe pain is a major challenge. When you have a significant injury, you're dealing with it 24/7. When the pain is severe enough to the point that your sleep is disrupted, your problems are compounded. People have a tremendous problem with fatigue when recovering. When you're severely injured and disabled, meaning you can't take care of yourself or your family the way you did before, it will be frustrating and possibly disheartening. Dealing with disability is difficult on all levels. Hopefully you're in a situation in which you will improve over time and return to your normal work and home status. A positive attitude is a must.

Another big challenge is having reduced or no income and mounting expenses. We need money to pay our bills. When you can't pay rent or mortgage and other bills, that is a struggle. We can assist in finding disability insurance you may have available through your own policies or through work. There also may be loan company options on a limited basis. We don't necessarily advocate for that, but we'll assist in the process of getting you at least some kind of short-term compensation.

The time that it takes to settle an injury claim can be a challenge. Cases can take many months, or even years in some instances. We know you just want the case over with and to be fairly compensated. When you're dealing with anything that is unknown, it can cause anxiety. For most people dealing with the insurance industry and the legal system, it's an unknown, so that fear can creep in. We are here to help you settle your fears.

Part of the claim process can involve the insurance company denying or questioning you. That is frustrating.

It is always frustrating when people deny something that we know to be true.

We are here to listen to you and counsel you through the process. If your case must be filed in court, you will have to give a statement known as a deposition. The defense attorney for the insurance company can be very offensive and very aggressive, but we will prepare you, be present with you and protect you. We work to make the process as effective and painless as possible.

What Happens if my Commercial Vehicle Accident CLAIM IS Denied?

Get a great attorney. You may want to talk to two or three attorneys to see how you feel with them. They should offer a no-obligation free consultation. You want to find someone who is capable, who has a proven track record and with whom you feel comfortable. You should feel confident and have a connection with the attorney. And, I suggest not signing any papers or giving any statements to insurance companies until you have had a legal consultation.

Compensation Recovered from A Commercial Vehicle Claim

You can seek to recover all of your "damages," which is the legal term for losses due to the incident. The two big damage categories are *economic* and *non-economic*. *Economic* losses are financial, like medical bills, income loss, medication, and devices such as crutches or wheelchairs. *Non-economic* losses are those things you feel and experience due to your injuries: the pain, suffering, disability, and disfigurement. Top-notch attorneys will work to get you full compensation for all of your losses.

Importance of an Attorney in Handling a Commercial Vehicle Claim

Insurance companies and the businesses they insure are experienced in the claims process and in litigation. They have vast resources. They are committed to paying as little as possible. You need someone to level the playing field for you - you need an advocate on your side.

Our mission is *maximum recovery in the minimum period of time*. Our strategy is to *plan, prepare and persist*. Each of those ingredients is necessary for a successful result. For your case, we will plan the case goals with you, we will prepare it in a proper way, and we will persist, even if things get difficult.

You can handle your case on your own but in my experience, 9 out of 10 times you won't be successful. You will have trouble not because you're not smart, tough or committed. It's because you don't know the rules, you don't have the resources and you don't have the wherewithal to succeed in litigation. Insurance claim procedures and legal processes are complicated. In some ways, the claims process is intentionally designed to frustrate you. You need a strong advocate in your corner.

UNINSURED / UNDERINSURED / HIT AND RUN MOTORIST CLAIMS IN ILLINOIS

Statistics show that one in seven drivers (13%) are uninsured. The statistics are based on studies by governmental and private research groups. What happens if you are hurt by an uninsured driver? You can get paid by making an uninsured motorist coverage claim.

Also, most drivers are *under*insured, which means they have insurance but they don't have high enough limits to cover serious injuries. I see it all the time in my law practice. People are seriously hurt and the other driver has minimal coverage of just $25,000 or $50,000.

Hopefully, if the other driver has low insurance limits, you have sufficient underinsured motorist coverage that is greater than your damages. At a minimum, you need $100,000 or more, even $250,000 or $1 million in underinsured motorist coverage.

The thing about underinsured motorist coverage is that we don't know if it is needed until we learn about the other driver's liability limits. In my experience, the vast majority of people have policies of only $20,000-$100,000 which is not enough insurance in cases of a serious injury. So, if you have a serious injury, and the other driver has less than $100,000 in liability coverage - they are underinsured.

With regard to your own uninsured and underinsured motorist coverage, *get high limits*. I encourage you to call your agent today to increase your limits. Higher limits are affordable. To double or triple your coverage is only a nominal increase in premiums. If your premium is $1,000 for $25,000 in coverage, to double your underinsured motorist coverage to $50,000 doesn't mean a premium increase to $2,000, it may be an increase of $100 or so.

It's a huge consumer disservice that insurance companies don't inform customers about the need and the low cost for additional coverage. My belief is that insurers do not want to have big exposure on high policy limits because the premium increases do not justify the exposure. Insurers don't tell people, "Well, for 25 bucks more, we'll double or triple your coverage," because it's not in their best interests. Their risk doubles or triples, but their income only increases a small amount. I've pushed for legislation to require insurer disclosure of the modest premium costs for massive coverage increases. It is an important consumer justice issue.

What if I'm Involved in an Auto Accident with an Uninsured Motorist?

If severely injured, medical attention is your first priority. Then get the police report. If the medical treatment is not urgently critical, get the police report at the scene.

You will be well served by getting a free, no obligation consultation with a competent uninsured motorist claim attorney.

After you speak with a capable attorney you can then notify the insurers yourself, or through your attorney, if you get good legal representation. If you contact the insurers yourself, do not give a statement or sign an authorization if you are going to retain an attorney. You could prejudice yourself.

It is important to record all of your experiences: keep copies of bills and records, photographs of the scene, the vehicle and your injuries. Write out "confidential attorney client" notes about how the injury affects you. Write out what pain you have including location,

description, intensity and duration. Note how you are

limited in daily activities. This information will help your attorney fully present your case.

We can monitor the traffic court proceedings against the uninsured driver. We go to traffic court with you, or for you, to make sure that the prosecutor and judge know that this driver is uninsured and that you were injured. This is important so that the negligent uninsured driver does not get off without consequences.

We also confirm the uninsured motorist's status with the Secretary of State. After the State confirms that the other driver is uninsured, they will move to revoke the license of that driver until payments are made. We also investigate any assets or income which the other driver may have.

We file a certified notice of claim and a Demand for Arbitration with your uninsured or underinsured motorist insurer. This notice is to protect your rights with regard to deadlines. Your auto insurance policy has a limitation period for filing claims and making the arbitration demand.

You are hopefully getting the medical care you need and you are documenting the effect of your injuries. Then, after you are recovered, we complete the process of compiling evidence of the incident and all of your damages. We consult with you to ensure we have complete information and then we discuss and agreed plan and goal.

We prepare and send a settlement demand package. Negotiations with your insurer begin and the claim will either settle or we will go to an arbitration, where we will pursue an award in your favor.

At some point shortly after the incident, you want to at least notify your insurance agent of the accident. I do not recommend giving a statement nor signing a document without having legal representation to handle the process. It is true that you can simply notify your insurer of the collision with another driver who had no insurance or had low policy limits.

Then speak to an attorney who can give you an initial free consultation on your rights and the process.

It is important to understand the difference between *notifying* your insurer of an incident versus *filing a claim*. The way insurance policies are written and the way insurance companies operate, it is critical to *notify* your insurer promptly of an incident. This notice is important, so they cannot later argue you did not provide notice and try to deny coverage.

You then make an uninsured motorist claim only when you have to - if the other driver does not have insurance.

If you are at fault in the accident, the other motorist will make a claim on your insurance company and they will handle it. Your insurance company will likely call you to ask you about the facts of the incident. Your cooperation is required.

DOES ILLINOIS REQUIRE UNINSURED MOTORIST COVERAGE?

Yes. The Illinois Insurance Code requires that uninsured and underinsured motorist coverage is provided in *every* auto liability policy. This means that every auto insurance liability policy must also have uninsured and underinsured motorist coverage.

Fortunately, the courts are somewhat inclined to rule in favor of consumers (as opposed to insurers) in the area of uninsured and underinsured motorist coverage.

It is one of the few areas where the consumer public has some protection from the courts against insurance companies.

What Does Uninsured Motorist Coverage Actually Cover?

Uninsured motorist coverage pays for all your injury related losses. Your losses or "damages" include *economic losses*, such as medical expenses and wage loss, and *non-economic losses* such as pain and suffering, disability and disfigurement.

Uninsured and underinsured motorist coverage is automatically included in your policy. Insist that your insurer provide a Declaration of Coverages that shows the dollar amounts of each coverage. These are your policy "limits." The Declaration is a page that will

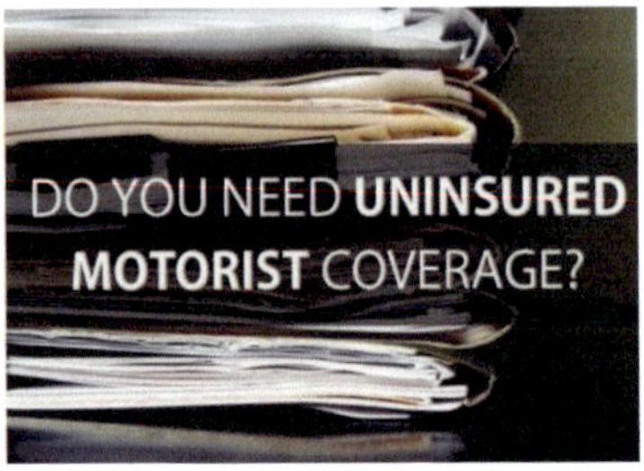

show your coverages and the limits of your coverage. The limits for your uninsured and underinsured motorist coverage must be equal to your liability limits. I strongly recommend that you have at least $100,000 in liability, uninsured, and underinsured motorist coverages. Ideally you carry $500,000 or more. My friend just increased his limits from $100,000 to $500,000 for just $14 a month!

Is it Advisable to Sue an Uninsured Person?

In certain circumstances, you may sue the uninsured person, but such a suit is usually not worthwhile. In the vast majority of cases, if a person drives without car insurance, they don't have assets (like a house or

savings or investments), and they don't have significant income. Even if you do sue the uninsured motorist, they usually file bankruptcy, which means you are barred from pursuing the lawsuit. In some cases, we have to sue the uninsured driver to protect the rights of your own insurance company in the event that we make an uninsured motorist claim.

How Do You Advise Clients Regarding a Lawsuit Against an Uninsured Motorist?

Most of us are taught from an early age to be responsible for ourselves and that if we break something, we have to fix it. Most of us conduct ourselves according to our own moral or ethical values.

If you are injured due to someone who is irresponsible (an uninsured motorist), it is frustrating. It is natural to be angry about someone who fails to have insurance and then causes injury. I hear it. I get it. It is wrong and unfair and irresponsible to drive without insurance. It is normal to be angry. However, what is your next positive useful step? An Uninsured Motorist Claim is your best course of action.

Life has many risks and we have few guarantees. However, we can protect ourselves against some risk. You do protect yourself with insurance coverage. That is the beauty of having uninsured or underinsured motorist protection. You can take steps to reduce the risks that are out there on the roadways.

What we do as lawyers for injury victims, is to work within the insurance and legal system, to get some form of justice for you. That justice may come about by monitoring traffic court proceedings to get fines and penalties against the other driver. We also work with state authorities in getting the uninsured motorist's license revoked until they make some form of restitution. And, ultimately we work to get financial compensation for your injuries.

That is my approach when representing my clients that have been injured by an uninsured motorist. It allows you to have some measure of peace of mind that something will be done to the at-fault uninsured driver.

Common Misconceptions Regarding Uninsured Motorists

One common misconception is that if you are injured by an uninsured motorist, you are out of luck. You do have a source of recovery, however, from uninsured motorist coverage.

Another misconception is that whether or not the other guy had insurance, the other driver must pay. Unfortunately, it's rare to be able to get someone without insurance to pay. Reasonable and responsible people have insurance.

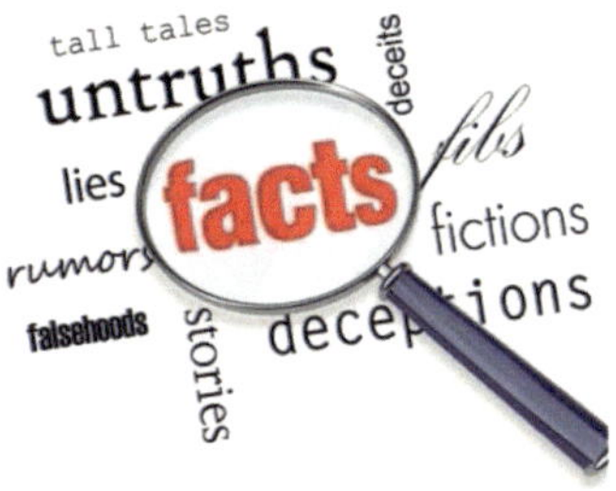

When somebody drives without insurance, they're neither reasonable nor responsible. And there is usually just no way to get them to pay because they have nothing to pay with. If they have some assets, they file bankruptcy to discharge their obligation.

There is another common misconception that I want to clear up. Many people are afraid to make a claim against their own insurance, because they think their rates will go up or they'll be dropped by their insurer.

However, in Illinois, the law prohibits insurers from increasing insurance premiums or dropping you if the accident is not your fault.

Of course, the legislature has put these laws in place because insurance companies are inclined to drop people who make a lot of claims or if they're in a lot of accidents. You paid for the insurance coverage and you need them now. Your insurer must pay you what they promised and what you purchased and they cannot increase your rates or drop you if you are not at fault.

Typical Outcomes of Uninsured Motorist Claims

We typically get excellent outcomes for our clients. Our guarantee is for very aggressive, experienced, and committed advocacy on your part. No honest attorney can guarantee a particular result. But we can guarantee we will fight for you. Much of my career has been built on being an attorney for people in uninsured and underinsured motorist cases.

I've handled hundreds of these cases for clients. I am also an arbitrator who hears and rules on uninsured motorist cases. An arbitrator is like a judge who hears the facts and listens to witnesses and attorneys on both sides. After the case is presented, the arbitrator makes an award. My experience as an arbitrator helps me in presenting cases as an attorney at arbitration. I typically get a good result for my clients.

I have also represented people where we made case law in the Illinois Appellate Court regarding underinsured motorist cases. One case involved a client who was on his bike and seriously injured by an underinsured motorist. His company (American Family) denied there was coverage. So, we went to the trial court and then the appellate court. We won in both courts. The insurer appealed to the supreme court but the supreme court refused to reconsider the rulings by the trial and appellate courts. So, we made law and we found coverage. The case was worth nearly half a million dollars. This was all after the insurance company denied coverage.

I'm also involved in getting the laws changed or amended so that they are more favorable to insurance consumers.

I've had three different pieces of legislation approved by the legislature and signed into law.

One law to do with arbitration awards for uninsured and underinsured motorist cases. Insurance companies want the right to reject those awards and make you go to the court. I've been successful in drafting amendments that were adopted into law that governs uninsured and underinsured motorist arbitration awards. If the award is under a certain amount, it is binding and cannot be rejected by the insurance company. I also drafted and supported the law that provides for penalties for improper insurance company delay and denial. We aggressively pursue a settlement or an arbitration award on every case and I would like the opportunity to help you with yours.

How are Hit and Run Accidents Classified in The State of Illinois?

A hit and run accident happens when a driver causes a collision and flees the scene. When someone causes an accident then leaves without identifying themselves, that's a hit and run.

Another type of incident that is classified as "hit and run" is when a vehicle part (e.g. a truck tire tread) from an unidentified vehicle comes off and causes an accident. Sometimes a tire tread or other vehicle part will go flying off a vehicle and cause damage. Because the drivers often don't know that happened, they continue driving, so they're unidentified, and that makes them a hit and run driver.

Common Misconceptions About Recovering Compensation After a Hit and Run or Uninsured Motorist Accident

The biggest misconception is that you are out of luck if you are injured in a hit and run accident. The truth is that you are fortunate if you have uninsured motorist coverage. If you've been injured by a hit and run driver, you have a remedy with uninsured motorist coverage.

If you've been involved in a hit and run accident and you're injured, first, get treatment. Whether you go to the emergency room, an urgent care clinic or your family doctor, get treatment. Safety first. If you're hurt, you have to see a doctor to rule out any serious condition.

If you're hurt and you don't see a doctor, the insurance company will say you're not hurt and not entitled to payment. They'll argue that in front of an arbitrator or judge or a jury, and many times, they win.

So, get the care that you need for your injuries, then collect all information about the incident, such as photographs, documents and the incident report. Your insurance company should be notified on a timely basis. If you do not notify them, you can lose your rights.

If you get an attorney, the attorney will pursue these items of proof for you. However, you have many items that the attorney can't get without you. So use a file folder, put everything in there and give the contents to your attorney. If your claim is of any significance, whether or not you get an attorney, I would highly recommend speaking to one. There should be a no-obligation free consultation available, so you don't have to pay anyone. Take an hour out of your week and become informed. Even if you decide not to hire an attorney - you have received free advice! And, if you handle the case on your own and it gets to be too much for you to handle, you know where you can go for legal representation.

Responsibility for A Hit and Run Accident in Illinois

Unfortunately, in a true hit and run accident, if the driver or owner of other vehicle is never identified, no individual is held responsible. It can be frustrating, but in terms of doing something effective, you make an uninsured motorist claim. Your insurance policy is a contract. You bought the coverage. It obligates your insurance company to pay you for your damages caused by the hit and run driver. You purchased this valuable protection, and you are entitled to the benefits if needed.

The Importance of Witnesses in Hit and Run Cases

Witnesses to a collision are important. Witnesses to a hit and run collision are even more important because we don't have the other driver to question about what happened.

The level of witness importance depends on the facts of the case. If you are rear-ended by a hit and run driver, other witnesses are not that important. However, if you lose consciousness and cannot testify about the collision, then you need other witnesses.

If you're stopped and you're hit from behind, the other driver is at fault. But if it's a collision in an intersection, and you're saying the other driver ran a light, it is very helpful to have a witness confirm that. Likewise, if you were knocked off the road by the hit and run driver, it's beneficial to have witnesses to confirm what the other driver did.

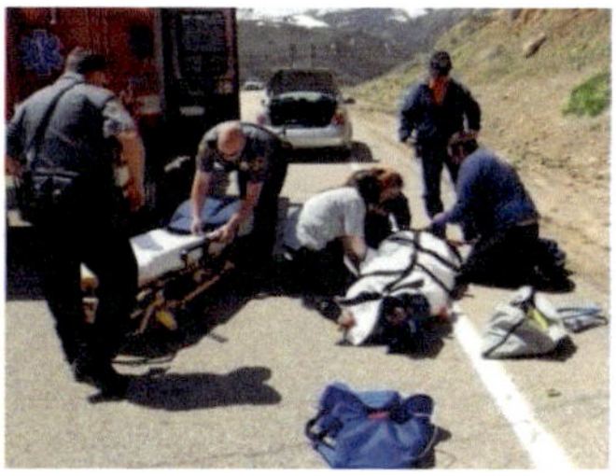

Witnesses are important, but they are not always essential. There are other forms of evidence, like physical damage. Damage to the rear of your car will suggest that you were rear-ended. Tire tracks on the roadway can also be evidence to suggest how an incident happened. All facts are potentially used as evidence and can be used in your favor to prove your case.

One of the definitions of "uninsured motorist" is hit and run driver. So when you're injured by a hit and run driver, the driver is considered "uninsured," and your uninsured motorist coverage applies.

Your insurance premium rate should not be affected if you're not at fault in a hit and run collision. Illinois law prohibits insurers from raising your rates if you're involved in a collision and you are not at fault.

We've often seen the at-fault driver claim to not have insurance, but after we start applying pressure to them by way of a written notice, certified mailings and phone calls, if they do have insurance, they'll eventually tell us. If they don't voluntarily do so, we'll file suit and get them to testify under oath as to their insurance status, but typically, in the early stages of the process, people will eventually tell us their insurance information.

IMPORTANCE OF RETAINING AN ATTORNEY FOR A HIT AND RUN CLAIM

You need an attorney because your insurance company is a powerful and experienced corporation. Insurers are experienced and skilled experts at delaying claims.

They are knowledgeable on legal rules and procedures. They have an army of insurance adjusters, claims personnel and lawyers who can delay your claim and deny you from getting fair compensation.

An experienced and capable attorney levels the playing field for you. He or she knows the rules, procedures, techniques and strategies that will help you get a maximum recovery in the minimum time.

When you're badly hurt, you have all sorts of stuff going on - you are in pain, you cannot get around, you're getting medical treatment, you're on medication, you're out of your routine, you cannot work, you can't be available for those who need you, you can't do housework, you can't exercise, you can't cook or clean, you can't do recreational activities and you can't do the simple things that make life worthwhile. It's really difficult to get your mind and heart around fighting an insurance company under those circumstances.

You likely need an attorney because the insurance company often will make a low ball offer to pay your medical bills and then maybe give you $1,000 or $5,000. The insurance company offer is usually not fair. The offer is usually not what you contracted for when you bought the policy. In our vast experience, after trying to handle cases on their own, people usually do get an attorney.

How Are Attorneys Compensated for Auto-Accident Claims?

You owe us nothing unless we recover for you. Our fee is based entirely on the amount of recovery that we get for you. Thus, we are driven to get you the maximum recovery in the minimum time. Our standard

fee is one-third of the recovery. If appropriate, we adjust our rate up or down if the case settles extraordinarily quickly or if early on the case goes through mediation or arbitration. Your case particulars are always subject to discussion and negotiation.

Scott Blumenshine Aggressively Handles Hit And Run / Uninsured / Underinsured Motorist Claims

You want someone who will get the best result and make the experience work for you. You need both information and guidance. When you've been injured and you have an insurance claim, it is often an unpleasant experience. We strive to make the best of it for you. We work to keep you informed, taken care of, advised, and well represented. We promise that. We can't promise a specific result. We can promise our every effort to get you the maximum recovery in the minimum time. Any lawyer who promises you a specific result is not telling the truth. We give you the truth, we give you information and we give you advocacy. We battle for you.

In the area of uninsured and underinsured motorist cases, I have been one of the most active attorneys in Illinois. I've represented hundreds of people with uninsured or underinsured motorist cases.

I am an arbitrator (judge) at arbitration hearings. I have written articles on the uninsured and underinsured motorist claims. I have written a book chapter on UM and UIM claims for practicing Illinois attorneys.

I am on the Insurance Law Section Council of the Illinois State Bar Association where I served on the Legislative Subcommittee. We review proposed insurance laws that will affect things like uninsured and underinsured motorist cases.

I am now Co-Chair of the Continuing Legal Education Committee of the Insurance Law Section. We arrange for expert attorneys in the area of insurance law to give presentations to other attorneys and inform them on insurance law topics and current strategies to succeed.

I have drafted and supported many pieces of legislation regarding uninsured and underinsured motorist coverage. I have also made some case law (judicial decisions) in the area.

It is my mission to help people with uninsured and underinsured motorist cases and I would truly enjoy the opportunity to serve you. Please call me for a free personal injury case consultation. I wish you the best.

Made in the USA
Monee, IL
05 November 2026

67386573R00050